A WORD IN
DUE SEASON

KENNESHA M. WALKER

A Word in Due Season
Copyright © 2021 Kennesha M. Walker

Published by
Ready Writer Press & Co.
P O Box 9703
Henrico, VA 23228
www.readywriterpress.co

Because of the dynamic nature of the Internet, any web addresses or links contained in this book may have changed since publication and may no longer be valid. The views expressed in the work are solely those of the author and do not necessarily reflect the views of the publisher, and the publisher hereby disclaims any responsibility for them.

ISBN (Paperback): 979-8-9962430-0-6
ISBN (Ebook): 979-8-9962430-1-3

Printed in the United States of America

Thank you, Lord, for loving me when I was down.
Thank you, Lord, for blessing me
when I didn't deserve the crown.
Thank you, Lord, for walking me
through the storms of life that toil.
Thank you, Lord, for changing me,
touching me with your anointed oil.
Thank you, Lord, for anointing me
to preach strongly in your name.
Thank you, Lord, for letting me know
that this life is not a game.
Thank you, Lord, for dying on the cross for me.
Thank you, Lord, for now my spirit has been set free.
For as many as the sands are upon the sea shore
And the stars that are in the sky-
Here are my many thank-yous,
for going on the cross to die.

Thank You, Lord
Adonai
Yeshua Messiah

CONTENTS

A SEASON OF CHANGE

What season does the leaves change to gold-
Where the soil is fertile,
Ready to receive the mysteries untold?
A seed sown to increase the anointing for our lives-
As we press toward the mark of the
High calling for the prize.

Changing our walk to stride as Yeshua did-
Dwelling in the secret place we abode and hid.
Hiding ourselves to spiritually grow in His name-
Yet letting our light shine so healing comes to the lame.

A light that shines through the summer,
A light that shines through the spring-
When autumn leaves start to fall,
Or when ice crystals begin to bring,
A shifting in the atmosphere,
An elevation of a spiritual song-
As orchestrated symphonies play
Melodies that echo long.

A cool calm breeze has run by,
Touching the surface of every face-
Changing our lives through Messiah,
God's Amazing Grace.
As we wait patiently as our season comes,
Our hearts begin to change-
To receive His Word and harvest
in this season of change.

WINTER

For as the rain cometh down, and the snow
from heaven, and returneth not thither,
but watereth the earth, and maketh it bring
forth and bud, that it may give seed
to the sower, and bread to the eater.

—Isaiah 55:10

As She Utters Her Voice

Deep and hidden sayings
Found interwoven in the wind
To begin
The Message from a feminine inflection

What does she have to say?
What is the message she holds?

Crying until she is heard
Tears of compassion
Tears of great joy
To employ the wailing
An overdue travailing
As she utters her voice

What does she have to say?
What is the message she holds?

Found deep within the womb
Carrying the Seed of Life
To break forth
And behold the Abrahamic covenant

A cry within the streets
On the top of high places
To stand and deliver The Message
As she utters her voice

A Zoë, life reflection
God's image-like connection
To the Earth
Now birthed out from the call
You have been chosen

Embroidered work of clothing[1]
Covered in the silk
Decked out
A crown of glory
Ornaments of grace and honor
To embrace
Yet, she gives it all to you
As she utters her voice

What does she have to say?
What is the message she holds?

Words of overflowing
Drip, drop
The outpouring
Of Holy Spirit in our souls
Words that drip like honey
Slowly saturating out whole being
Now believing, then seeing
As she utters her voice

Wisdom

---

1   Ezekiel 16: 10.

'TWAS THE NIGHT BEFORE THE INCREASE

'Twas the night before the increase,
And the praises each person did uphold-
For the hour was at hand to prosper,
Increase from brass and iron to silver and gold.
The worship was high for God was there to see-
That His people wanted to move
forward in His purpose,
That was prophesied early in the ministry.

The children were excited
To get what God had for them-
For He wrote out the vision for them to pursue it,
Not the world, but of Him.

Then inside of the congregation,
there arose such a midst-
We sprang from our seats and proclaimed happy bliss.
Away to the altar we flew like a flash-
Some moved like lightning, others in a quick dash.

With all that was going on,
Everything just seemed to fit-
We knew at that moment, it must be Holy Spirit.
More rapid than eagles, His angels they came-
Yet, in the midst of it all, He called us by name.

"For you are holy, magnificent, wonderful, and kind-
Redeemed, saved, anointed, such a brilliant mind.
To the top of your head to the soles of your feet-
I have set the time for you to move forward,
Now Satan is at defeat."

As we lifted up our hands to get what was in store-
God opened the floodgates and sent down an outpour.
An outpour of miracles, blessings,
prosperity just the same-
Growing with the anointing,
God's gift we did proclaim.

There were parcels of spiritual gifts,
He had abiding in midair-
For all we had to do was reach for it,
Then it would be ours to share.

For one was given by the Spirit the word of wisdom,
Another the word of knowledge by the same-
Another the gift of healing,
Faith, prophecy, just some others to name.
For one the working of miracles,
To another discerning of spirits-
To another diverse kinds of tongues,
And the interpretation that fits.[2]

---

2   1 Corinthians 12:8–10.

Then He spoke not a word,
But moved throughout this place-
And filled all of our hearts with His love,
And His amazing grace.
And laying His hand on all of our lives-
Giving us the joys of our purpose as our hearts revive.

But we all heard Him proclaim
as the mist left out sight-
"Go forth in my Word,
My anointing has increased you on this very night."

THE SIGNATURE, WORD

Cursive writing, messages
Blocked letters, things in print
Verbal, written signatures
He, the Word was sent
To address the waiting
For the written saying that speaks of He
Read on
Read on
Going deep into understanding
Three hours before dawn
An internal passion to feed upon the Alef Tav Berit
Covenant written scrolls on animals
In Him, we are complete
The fullness of all that God is
In union, we are made[3]

---

3   Colossians 2:8–9, CJB.

Gathered together
We stand, under shadow and shade
We hear the sound like thunder
At meah four and thirty-two
On sabbatical day before the sun
Breathe out CO_2
We thirst to know
Through the scrolls and special ink
The name above names
Hidden from the world
Yet, we pause in time to unwind
To rest and take shalom
The peace in Him
Signed and sealed
Until the Revelation

THE BATTLE WITHIN

Ready, Aim, Fire,
Shoot for the victory,
For the soul is a battlefield.
To cross that line of deception and pain-
To gather up joy, happiness, the anointed rain.

Look up yonder, see the enemy in sight-
Gathering his imps and demons,
It will be a battle, yet we will fight-
Fight against evil rulers, authorities,
Against the powers of the dark world,
Against the spiritual forces of evil
in the heavenly realms.[4]

Putting on the armor of God,
To resist the devil in every which way we can-
Using the sword, the Bible,
To sever the word of the carnal man.
Using the helmet of salvation,
To show a change in one's life-
Using the shield of faith,
To quench all fiery darts that penetrate like a knife.

---

4   Ephesians 6:10–18, NLT.

Shodding one's feet with the preparation
Of the gospel of peace-
Having the truth that girds our loins and the
breastplate of righteousness to war against every
demonic beast.

For the soul is a battlefield
And who shall win has been
Determined before it did begin-
For God has won every soul
Through the battle within.

Inquiring Minds Would Like to Know

Inquiring minds would like to know
What really makes you tick-
When people talk bad about you or when you're sick?

Inquiring minds would like to know
What really makes you smile-
When people turn up their noses
When you go that extra mile?

Inquiring minds would like to know
What really makes you glow-
They see that there's something different about you,
Tell them, they want to know.

Inquiring minds would like to know
What really makes you sing-
You sing without harmonious melodies,
A rhythmic beat or string?

Inquiring minds would like to know
What must they do to get this?
This is something they want as well,
To live in happy bliss.

I'll tell you, my friend, what's in store
For those who seek His name
It's oh so quite simple really-
Don't seek after the world's fashion and fame.

Jesus, Yeshua, died on Calvary
To save our sin-sick souls-
He rose up on the third day, my friend,
And took all our strongholds.

Blessed be that know Him for
He is great in every way-
Because thou shalt forget thy misery,
And remember it as waters that pass away.[5]

I love to see people who seek after
God's most perfect will-
I have so much compassion for them
That my heart just won't keep still.

Nobody told me the road would be easy
And I will tell you the same-
At some point in your Christian walk,
You will have to call on His name.

---

5   Job 11:16.

Your adversary, the devil, as a roaring lion, walks about,
Seeking whom he may devour-[6]
But remember that God has not given us a spirit of fear
But of love, a sound mind, and of power.[7]

This road is rough, I tell you, it isn't a piece of cake-
You have to take the good with the bad,
Right down to every mistake.

It's better to suffer as a Christian
For your blessings come through much pain-
The pain for acknowledging Him as your Savior
And the level of your spiritual gain.

I know why I sing without harmonious melodies,
A rhythmic beat or string-
Because Jesus gave me the victory,
Through Him I can do anything.

I know why I can do all things through Christ
With such a pleasant smile-
Because He saved me when I was lost,
When He went that extra mile.

I know why I shine so bright, bright with such a glow-
Because Jesus is the focus of my life; tell them…

…Inquiring minds would like to know

---

6   1 Peter 5:8.

7   2 Timothy 1:7.

SHED A TEAR

To shed a tear for one or even shed a tear for two-
The pain you felt all this time
When the world turned its back on you.
The upsets and disappointments that you received
During times of your ancient past-
Yet God is looking at your heart,
You will finish first and not at last.

Your trials are just a stepping-stone
To receive the full anointing on your life-
Breaking the chains of bondage
To destroy all matter of strife.
However, there was a man that cried aloud,
When He went upon the cross-
To set the captives free from all danger
So no soul would be lost.

He cried aloud, showing He cares for us
Crucifying His flesh to give life, liberty
Abundant blessings as in a trust.
Oh, the agony He felt
When they pierced Him in His side-
Blood and water seeping down his bod
Giving life as he cried.

Cried as a mother laboring, who gives birth to a child-
Bringing forth a new spirit that is holy, meek, and mild.
He feels your hurt in every step,
As you walk upright in His way-
To uphold the good and not evil,
Soon the night will turn to day.

For the darkest hour is before the morning light,
That shimmers in the sky-
Palm trees that blow wildly in the wind
That bow down to the Most High.

Everything does worship Him
For He is everywhere so near-
So draw closer to that very one
To whom shed a tear.

TO TURN BACK THE HANDS OF TIME

If you could turn back the hands of time,
What would you really do?
Would you have stopped the madness
And gotten yourself right?
To refresh your mind anew?

Anew toward Jesus, Yeshua, Heaven just along the way,
Yet you waited too late to get it right before this day.
Oh, if the hands of time could be turned about,
What would you really do?
Would you have given your life to Christ,
So His rest could follow through?

Worship and praise were the keys of your success,
But all has faded away,
Now you're rotting in a fiery pit
In what…I don't want to say.

See, time is so precious,
There is no time to waste,
Give your life to Jesus and the rest will come in haste.
For His mercy endures forever
And there is much reward for doing right,
For He loves you with all of His heart
So just walk into His light.

Eyes Wide Shut

I'll let this go
And start this new flow
By a gesture
Or some hypothetical sound
That echoes to follow
Where it can be found
Like a key to a treasure,
But the path unknown
Until it is shown by a lamp to my feet
Yet, if I turn from its side
And follow a winding road
What can explode in my face
Could turn to my grace
I find myself back on the road where I belong

Can you speak with words?
Can you confess what's not said?
Can you make a joyful noise -
When you are sleep in the bed?
Sleepy…but not asleep.

Will it turn out to be like an armed man, your need?[8]
Or will your multiply your seed
Or will you have a talent minus one.

But what does it mean, "I see,' said the blind man?"
Stand and ponder these words
Selah

Your naked eye can see, but can your heart comprehend
Eyes see, but don't see
So does that mean eyes are wide shut?

No faith—that's the mean

---

8   Proverbs 24:34.

SPRING

The flowers appear on the earth; the time of the singing of birds is come, and the voice of the turtle is heard in our land; The fig tree putteth forth her green figs, and the vines with the tender grape give a good smell. Arise, my love, my fair one, and come away.

—Song of Solomon 2:12–13

THE WAY OF LOVE

An uttered sound, words encrypted
Understood by no man
Like an instrument of brass, tinkling in its sound[9]
Could be an itching of the ear[10]

But we look towards what's just and true
His ways are not our ways
His thoughts, not our thoughts[11]

But like a Hammond played
Harmonic melodies, vocalized that say
Love's in need
For what?
You imply
Love replies back in her echoing call
She cries out no more in the streets and high places
At the entry of the heart
At the coming in at the gates

For more can be expected from unfailing
It's penetrating and prevailing
The heart's mind to see His grace

---

9   1 Corinthians 13:1.

10   2 Timothy 4:3.

11   Isaiah 55:8.

When He comes, what's so darkly seen departs
Then face to face being[12]
What she has been seeing
Our expected end

---

12   1 Corinthians 13:12.

Just Imagine

Oh, just imagine how it would be, a ball. You have been rushing through the whole day to make it to this engagement. It seems as though, throughout all the turn of events that lead to turmoil, whatever happened dissipates and liquefies when you arrive at the ball. Once you enter in, a well-defined cordial gentleman greets you and escorts you to a seat. So far, you and the gentleman are the only ones there. You feel as though you can talk to him about anything and thus the story begins…

HAVE YOU EVER?

The gentleman speaks so calmly to say-
"Hello, my lady, how was your day?"
You are filled with such sorrow, such worry, and pain-
That the tears roll down your face for
That's all you could contain.

"I've been hurting inside so long, it's true-
That my life seems like it's coming to an end,
I just don't know what to do."

He takes you by the hand and says,
"It is going to be okay-
Joy comes in the morning,
You will make it through this day."

"Maybe you're right, what have I to lose-
I mean, I've been hurt so many times,
Ok, that is what I choose."
As you made your choice, you thought on some things-
This man is genuine; He knows what the future brings.

As you contemplate on those
things He said even further,
You think, "This man is real;
Come on, girl, have you ever?"

Have you ever met a man
That would sweep you off your feet?
Have you ever met a man
Who would whisper your name so sweet?
Have you ever met a man so cordial and so kind?
Have you ever met a man with such a brilliant mind?

Have you ever met a man so humble and so meek?
Have you ever met a man?
Hey, this is what I seek.

As you embrace in a hug He says,
"I have something for you-
Eternal life with God, Jesus Christ, He is what's true."

"Who is this Jesus to whom I must seek-
Is He as wonderful as you,
So temporal and meek?"

"I could not enter in where I was unwanted-
You opened your heart to Me,
It shows you are undaunted.
I met you at the door, I ushered you in-
I brought peace to your mind and spirit,
Through Me you can win.

But you are a chosen generation, royal priesthood[13]
of high maintenance-
Let Me formally introduce myself,
I'm Jesus Christ, your Savior,
Glad to make your acquaintance."

---

13   1 Peter 2:9.

ONE MISTAKE

It was just one mistake I made
And Satan has me down,
He said, "You are a good for nothing thing you,
For that I'll keep you bound.

I'll tell you that you are worthless,
I'll tell you that there is no end-
To the emptiness and loneliness,
Oh, all Hell will break in.

I'll make you feel like an ant buried
Deep within sinking sand
You can't breathe, you can't get out
There is no one to lend a hand.

For you made one mistake and ain't that the truth-
I'll keep on making you think that
God does not love you,
And I surely have the proof.

You made just that one mistake and
God has turned His back on you-
Why would He have let you do that thing,
I thought He really loved you.

Ain't it a shame, you have to live
With it for the rest of your life-
You might as well keep sinning because
bitterness will turn to strife.

Ha, ha I got you beat; I got you to turn away-
I knew God had a mighty plan set for you,
But it made you stop so you wouldn't pray."

"Well, I'll tell you this one thing, Satan,
I have just had enough of you-
I am sick and tired of hearing your mouth,
I am fed up with your little games too.

You are immature, deceitful,
A pathological liar all the time-
You just get on my nerves I tell you,
Leave me alone so I can worship The Divine.

For I know that I cannot stay fixed within this low-
So then, I must repent for my sins
And move with a spiritual flow.

God's grace will come upon me,
And I'll know that everything's okay-
God's got my back even though
I made a mistake that day.

I have repented and moved on,
My life you can't have anymore-
As of now, get behind me, Satan
For God's bringing me an outpour.

See, God really does care for me,
He speaks to me softly, I'm able to hear-
Echoing so lovely, so crystal and clear.

For it is perpetual, moving forward,
Pushing without end-
God yet knows the ending before it will begin.

So you see, if I made just one mistake,
God knows the deal-
He knows whatever you throw up at me,
I will recover what you steal.

For this one thing I tell you,
My life to God I take-
To Him who forgave me when I
repented for that one mistake."

Appreciate It

Have you ever said "Thank you" when someone
Reached out their hand
To help you make a change in your life-
A change that saved you from going down
The path of destruction and pain-
A path that would have killed
Your character, personality, and spirit-
A spirit of everlasting peace, a joy of living each day
waking up to something different, something
unexpected and new?

What motivates you to do what you do?
Are you led by a mind of confusion or
A steadfastness in the Spirit?

Holy Spirit

Do you uphold God's Spirit of Love, Joy, Peace,
Longsuffering, Meekness, Temperance, Gentleness,
Goodness, and Faith?

Appreciate what God has given you, for it is yours.
Appreciate what God has done,
Letting His only begotten Son die for your sins.

In writing this, my heart cries out
For God really cares for you.
He went out of His way
To organize such a plan to get you closer to Him.

He is merciful.

The warmth of His presence
Has summer evenings lit with star twinkles
With cool, calm breezes
That hit the shore that seem like nothing.

His presence cannot be compared
to the tender brush of
Scented roses, white pearl diamonds,
golden white dreams,
Or even a kiss on the hand on
a summer night's bliss.
He is in a category all His own.

Appreciate what God has given you to treasure
dearly. Nurture and let it grow.
Feed your soul a cup of love,
A dash of praise, a pound of mercy,
A pinch of grace and a handful of patience.

Appreciate what God has given you.
He gave you His Spirit to show others the way.
Your soul lights up like a firefly,
In the darkness, your emphasis is made known.

Your day brightens
With the heavenly sunlight that burns with
A passion, a yearning to move closer, and closer.

What is that glimmer?
So internal, so invisible, so magnificent, so appetizing,
A hunger to eat of this very Vine,
A relationship with Yeshua—Jesus.

A marriage, a bond
An everlasting feeling of happiness
Once empty, now full
Can only be cherished with your one true love,
Your love for Yeshua.

Appreciate It

What Can It Be?

What can it be?
It's a mystery
The tongues speaking of the Unknown
In a Groan
Moan
That is Sown
The natural man perceiving
Not what's spoken
A token, which opens
The windows of heaven
With a light burning bright
Out of sight
Pure delight
In His presence

But…
What can it be?
It's a mystery

Speak up
Say, what?
There's something that I heard
Splurge
Surge
Into the deep things of God
His Spirit, my spirit becoming one
His only Son
Dying on the cross for me
Don't you see?

The first has been broken
Therefore, we are soaking
In His ecstasy
Coming to round two
Let me through
So that I may taste of the Vine

But…What is mine?
Everything I say,
Portray,
Arrange,
Array
But what can it be?
Though I speak a mystery
The perfect wisdom of God
Hidden from the world's princes
Using all senses
To steal kill and destroy

But what senses do you use?
Because the naked eye cannot see

Nor the ear can perceive
What's in store for His children
But what can it be?
Can you receive, believe
On His report?
Intensify
Unify
Such things that are sought?
Bought with a price
The ultimate sacrifice
Now, how do you like that?

A language not like binary
To a hacker breaking a code
Can only listen
To the encryption
Having great faith on how I flowed
To the Father
Only He knows what it can be

It's Morning

Have you seen the clouds go by
On a peaceful evening so dim?
Have you seen the clouds take pictures
of evening days so grim?
Have you heard the thunder clap its hands,
To show forth its strength and might?
Have you heard the thunder sing a
tune that whispered in the night?

I wonder what is in store
Once this storm passes through–
I wonder what is in store once dark skies
Turn to yellow, orange, pink, and blue?

The day dawns great wonders,
Unexpected things that God has to give away–
Things that are righteous, precious, and are in array.

It's morning and I will arise,
Taking up my bed to walk–
Days long of righteousness shall my tongue talk.[14]

14   Psalm 71:24a.

Speaking boldly in His name
To proclaim what He will and has done-
Moving mightily through the Spirit of God
To give Word about His Son.

God uses many people to spread the Word
To whom are believers-
Believers whom He gave some
Apostles, prophets, evangelists, pastors, and teachers.[15]
As the daybreak creeps low and
descends below the crescent dust-
I know that my work is not finished,
for I must move on, I must.

For when I awake from my dormant sleep
And arise to something new-
I'll say when the sun rays hit my windowpane,
"It's morning, Jesus, and I will give it all to you."

---

15   Ephesians 4:11.

Still Waters

Panes of glass dripping with tears
A cry of subtle hope
Pain, agony, a yearning for comfort
A stretch of hands towards the sky

Surrendering all both spirit and soul
As an hart panteth after the water brooks   *(Psalm 42:1)*
The ocean waves strike the line
Then retreat to their domain

Moving rapid, creeping slow
Swaying back and forth
Painted rivers as rippling mirrors
Calling perpetually until heard

Contained as a clay pot
Holding its substance
Covering it inward parts
Hovering over the water
Touched, kissed, protected, and loved

Its lid is removed
Let it rain
So it may be filled with the newness of joy

Who giveth rain upon the earth?   *(Job 5:10)*
Who sendeth waters upon the fields?

Psalm 33:7 Who gathereth the waters of the sea together
as an heap
And layeth up the depth in storehouses?
Never to be tainted
Revelation 22:1 Clear as crystal
He moves upon the waters
He refreshes the soul
He restores strength through weakness

Calm as the seas
Never moved
Never flustered

Shh…
Rest at Yeshua's feet
Lie down in His green pastures
Teardrops of honey melting into a fragrance
of frankincense and myrrh

Shh…
Unfailing springs
An unquenchable fire that sparks the waves

Shh…
Fertile soil with an outpour of joy

The waters of quietness
Hovering over every being
Resting in His bosom
Still in Heavenly Peace

TIME

Time is of the essence
Time can be so pure

Time
Star-fire lit
Pure vision as candles
Time has no limit of what you can bear
In the bosom of His sweet happiness
that can lift you in the air

Time
Age can be defying once you see it through
With Yeshua by your side,
You'll have eternal life without end,
Continuous blessings
In addition to

Time
I know who makes my day bright
Bright with a heavenly whirlwind
Of magnificent sunlight
I wonder what the day may bring from His loving grace
The move of the Holy Spirit lighting this place

His Spirit is oh so precious
Precious as the sweet rolling mist
That plagues my body with His sweet, adoring bliss

Days I have wondered here below
How on earth did I deserve Him so?
He came down from heaven to take back the night
Taking back what the devil stole
Which was perfectly set in His sight

The time has not come until now
Now, it is time

To everything there is a season
For what is next, is all the reason

There is a time to be born, a time to mourn
A time to plant and pluck up
A time to cast away and gather stones
A time to break down and build up

There is a time to kill, a time to heal
A time to laugh and weep
A time to hate, a time for peace
A time to war, let silence keep

There is a time to die, a time to dance
A time to love, and cast away
A time to embrace in turn refrain from
That which cannot stay

There is a time to get, a time to lose
A time to also speak
And then a time to rend and sew
A time to also keep[16]

For everything that God has, everything has a function
Find out what your purpose is
So you can function under His unction

Nevertheless, at this time,
God has blessed us through His Son
For He shalt arise, and have mercy upon Zion:
For the time to favour her, yea, the set time, is come[17]

16   Ecclesiastes 3:1–8.
17   Psalm 102:13.

A ROSE

A rose is a rose that is planted to bloom,
Petals of multiple colors,
Yellow, orange, pink, and blue.
To plant a seed brings life to all,
Touching its surroundings,
Be they great or small.

The weather changes to a wintry cold
As withered leaves come to pass,
It goes through pain, sorrows that hurt so,
But they surely never last.
As the weather changes once more to a moisture,
A warmth that is set so high,
This withered flower then lifts its head
As it reaches towards the sky.

For that's where the strength comes from,
From the Lord who is so true,
He holds you in the palm of His hands
As He molds you into something new.
So as your life seems rough at times
And the pain seems hard to bear,
Remember, you are going to blossom, my dear-
A rose made perfect to care.

THE SHIFT

Who will hear His voice speak plain,
To change their season
From drought to rain?

The summer heat is blazin'
God's grace is so amazin'
To break the po folk chain
To change our drought to rain
His Word is just like fire
To lift us even higher

Can you contain it?
No room to receive it
Busting out, can't fit it
The anointing transmitted
An ATM transaction
What you see is just a fraction
To the whole equation
Add and multiplication

For He said I will multiply thee[18]
You and your seed
Exceeding abundantly
Above all we can ask or think[19]
So just blink

---

18   Genesis 22:17.
19   Ephesians 3:20.

Bat your eyes,
Go to Sleep
Wake up, wake up
It's time to reap!

Tick, tock, It's your hour
To receive your might and power
To His people, hidden treasure
NOW faith beyond measure[20]

Can you so believe it?
Catch it and receive it?
Walk in new beginnings?
With Him a never-ending
To the story told
Pure as fine gold

We already made that switch
From poor to richie rich
We got it
We got it

Rain, rain, come today
Come again every day
Drip, drop, let it pour
He'll increase you more and more

20   Hebrews 11:1; Romans 12:3.

It's like fire shut up in our bones
Gifts of precious stones[21]
In the eyes of Him, burn bright
Out of DARKness
Into His marvelous light

---

21   Proverbs 17:8.

SUMMER

For he shall be as a tree planted by the waters,
and that spreadeth out her roots by the river, and
shall not see when heat cometh, but her leaf shall
be green; and shall not be careful in the year of
drought, neither shall
cease from yielding fruit.

—Jeremiah 17:8

His Wings

He spreads abroad His wings
And soars above the mountaintops

He wraps me in His love
Keeping me safe from all harm[22]

He overshadows with the fullness of joy
Found within His presence

My beloved has arisen, nurturing my wounds
with the healing in His wings[23]

---

22   Psalm 91:4, Psalm 121:7&8.
23   Malachi 4:2.

IMPRINTS OF HEAVEN

Imprints of Heaven
Have fallen afresh on my mind
Imprints of Heaven
Just happened to let me find
That Jesus is the source of every divine

Power and force that controls my ways
Long-lasting hope and glory in all of my days

Salvation and Deliverance
Charity and Peace
Joy and Gladness
Are needed the most, not least

Imprints of Heaven
Give me something to look for
Continuous praise toward Jesus
For that's what's in store

In store for what I'll see once I cross that line
To see the kingdom of God manifest
As I enter eternity and step out of time

Imprints of Heaven
Feed into my spirit and soul
To pursue good not evil
To suppress the battle and achieve my goal

My goal of searching what God has for me
Searching those imprints of heaven in heaven
To magnify Him continuously

Imprints of Heaven

His Por to Fill

Dust and gravel, granite
Dirt, twigs, and sand
Things that formed human nature
Physical formation that God called man
Together with the water
To form a mixture
To captivate His nature

From the Potter comes His Por

The clay is formed by purpose
Refined within the fire
As the metal pieces of silver and gold
Ready to be sold for the Master's use

A vessel sanctified and honored
A treasure found in Adam
The rib to form the same
A name of the mother travailing to bring forth life

A ministry ordained by purpose
Having been called
Having been chosen to do
Through wells of overflowing
springs of life that subdue
A thirst of the quenchable fire
A burning for the Word

From the mountains to the valleys
The rivers and the seas
The cliffs and the treetops
Desert sands and the streams

From the Potter comes His Por

The filling of the soul
The story untold of the newness of joy
Until now
An outpour of His blessings
Overflowing from within
To begin a new life without strife
Shekinah glory filled
The never-ending story
Perpetually calling is now heard
To fulfill the purpose of His vision

Pick Up Your Face

Pick up your face from off the ground
and wear it with great pride
Joy and gladness come from above.

Know This
That all things work together for
good to them that love God,
To them who are the called according to his purpose[24]

Although you do your best and stick
with God's plan to the end,
And when you are praised through
the people who love,
But they don't do what is placed on their lives

Keep Striving
Because
Whereunto I also labor,
Striving according to his working,
Which worketh in me mightily[25]
For I know that things will come together

I know that ye are complete in him,
Which is the head of all principality and power[26]

---

24   Romans 8:28.

25   Colossians 1:29.

26   Colossians 2:10.

Hold Up!
Maybe that's not all to your circumstance

You need to be encouraged
I pray that God will keep you in perfect peace
Calm as the evening that bears
the beginning of blessed quietness
An inner peace

Ocean waves tap musical notes upon the seashore
Birds singing joyous lullabies of
He loves me, He loves me
Regardless of my circumstances
Regardless to what I am faced with on a daily basis
Regardless to the trials and tribulations
Regardless to what lies in my path
Regardless to the judgmental decisions
of inaccuracy that I make
He loves me

Pick up your face from off the ground
and wear it with dignity
Yeshua will guide your every footstep
Through the storm

Be blessed for your spirit is of His
and He delights in you
Walk in the newness that
He has predestined for you to have
Stay focused on His will and His purpose
He has written the vision for you to pursue it
It will not plunge so,
Pick up your face and stand fast in His Word

Hello, How Are You?

Do I need to lend a hand?
Do you really need a friend?
I am at your beck and call
I'll be there to help you when you fall

Do you know who made the oceans roar?
Do you know who made the birds
spread their wings to soar?
Do you know who made the sea so blue?
Do you know who made the trees
bow down when the wind blew?
Do you know who has the power
to right whatever is wrong?
Do you know who has the power
to make you strong?
Do you know that my yoke is easy
and my burdens are light?
Do you know that my plan for you
is mightily set in my sight?

I can't bear not knowing how you feel
I can't bear not knowing if you
know that I am really real
I would really love to hear from you
If you have any problems with the
things you are going through
Let me make myself very clear
I want to be in the midst of whatever you fear
I want to be able to hold you near
I want you to be the wheel that I steer

Do you feel okay?
Just kneel down and pray
I'll heal you from your pain
There are blessings that you will gain

Just stay under my will
You will go far if you stand still
I will direct your path
Regardless of the aftermath

You are my child and I love you so
I would really like to see you grow
I am the wind beneath your wings
I want to take care of you above all things

Have you ever wondered
What is on the other side of the door?
Have you tried to open it,
Peek through to see what's in store?
Have you wondered
What's in it for you if you had a key?
Have you ever wondered
What you could do if you set your spirit free?

Please don't worry, don't be so tense
Hello, how are you?
I am your Lord, Savior, and Prince

What Is It All About?

I cry in silence for He has pierced my soul
With His marvelous light
He plagues my body with the joys
And wonders of His treasures
He has stored up for me

He entices me to move forward
To His calling, His purpose, His being
The Christ-like characteristics
And attributes that reveal
Quiet blissfulness, overwhelming joy
A craving of His Word
A thirst for knowledge and understanding
…
Wisdom

He charms me with His compassion,
His grace and mercy
For the Lord loves me unconditionally,
Everlasting, without end
I may hold sorrow, pain, agony, fatigue,
But God can wipe the slate clean
With His Spirit nurturing and protecting me
Holding onto His unchanging hand
for He died in my place
Making me strong through Him
With all, I can work miracles or even heal the sick

His warmth fills my soul with
righteousness, sovereignty, and love
He surrounds me with His angels that guard
My every move, my every step, my every motion

He sets my feet on holy ground
None of quickening sand, but of a moisture
Of calm and quiet seas
Blessed and orchestrated songs
The birds sing within the trees
An ocean spray of love and an abundant livelihood

I am anchored in the Lord
I am etched in stone
My feet are planted in His Word
The fertile soil of my spirit and soul
I will not turn back
For He has brought me from a mighty long way

Why turn back and be infested
with the lust of the flesh?
Why glorify the physical being when God has given
Provision, Sanctification, Unity,
A bond,
A covenant that if I worship Him,
He will get the glory and honor
. . .
The Praise and Worship

I will be loosed of my problems,
My strongholds, and infirmities
Why dwell in such perverseness, such manipulation?
For all leads to destruction
An everlasting hellfire

An anguish of a never-ending death,
A mind of insanity,
An imprisonment of torture,
A captive of my own lusts of infidelity
Trapped

Hardening not my heart to what has been said

Blessed is the man that walketh not
In the counsel of the ungodly.[27]
Calling on His name, for surely He will be there
Blessed Be the Lord

---

27   Psalm 1:1.

Singled Out

By myself, I stand
As some of you do too
With no cares of another
Well, maybe, sisters and brothers in Christ
But that's it!

Don't misconstrue if it's morning two
Not doing anything wrong
Just hanging with my crew—of friends
Let it be known
It's Praise, Worship, and the Word
You know…that Zoë livin' to its very potential

Yet, in a crowd, I stick out
Like wearing red to a bull
A target to the enemy
A magnet to prosperity
That draws me to my destiny

The cover—His crimson blood
It washes the filth and mud of the past
That cannot stay nor last
Nor cross over the line to what's new

But I'm not through
See, I'm being worked on—from the inside out
Coming up from absurdity
Without a shadow of a doubt
I will be as my heart sees me
Like the Word poured into a cup
It overflows my whole being
Then
Conceiving the believing
A reflective image of the Word
Dividing what's absurd
By being singled out

The Sky

As you all know
The saying goes
"The sky's the limit"
But what does that mean
For something that's seen
Visible to the eye?

To my surprise
I caught a revelized notion
Between the space and the ocean
What we believe there is no cap
To our ability
—A no-faith trap
To such a phrase we grasp not a clue.

Let me explain…

We see it as a limitless entity
"The sky" beyond natural ability
That we may rest in its sanction
—Tranquility
But our feet are planted ashore

No more do we move toward that
Rocket ship or climb beyond our reach
We beseech
but never do

Seeing both sky and stars
Thinkable, yet unreachable
—It seems so far

The separation of sky and space
An atmospheric combustion to time and grace
We face to fail by natural circumstances
Taking mundane wisdom to justify spiritual advances
By God's grace He can do exceeding above what
we think
Far over and above all, before our eyes can blink

In a twinkle
It's reachable
Superabundantly
Infinitely
Beyond our highest prayers, desires, thoughts, hopes,
and dreams
Clichés, seek no more
Of such oral literature,
Superstitious folklore

By one Book you got the key
So use it responsibly
And see
That between the space and ocean
Lies a cap to devotion
With phrases that have an ending

By His Words we are beginning to see
—Through Ephesians 3 and twenty…

…that the sky is a LIMIT.

SMILE

I know that things may bother you,
At times, there is no end-
Every time you look around,
You see the trouble rolling in.

Mind filled with confusing thoughts,
Thoughts that cannot see you through-
Through the problems, heartaches,
and tears you have cried,
Because of what's troubling you.

I know of things that have blessed peace,
Peace, Overwhelming joy,
Joy that you can have
Once you know that He is always there.

I find happiness through my sorrows,
I find happiness through the rain-
I find happiness in every morrow,
When the sunrays hit my windowpane.

I love things that are pleasing to Him,
That touch my heart so sore-
Loving what God has made has given me,
Eternal gladness all the more.

Throughout all of your heartaches and pains,
I know who can see you through-
No matter what the problem is,
God holds dear to you.

Give it to Him and leave it there
And watch that seed manifest,
Manifest into grapevines,
Vines of fruit,
Overflowing with aquatated dewdrops,
Blessings that you have received.

Received, for that I can smile
Smile, for your smile is contagious-
Smile, to help someone overcome and make it-
Smile, when things don't go your way-
Smile, when darkness tries to overcloud you day-
Smile

For these things that I speak
Have been a blessing unto me-
A blessing to my spirit and soul,
To overcome adversity.
What to say now?
Hmmm…
Let me see-
I pass this on to you that you may be blessed indeed.
Smile

Interwoven Pieces

Interwoven pieces
Sown together with a needle and thread,
Intricately knitted
Arrayed in beauty when God said

Let us make man in our image[28]
Fearfully and wonderfully made
Wrought our inward parts
Under the shadow
In the shade[29]
Developed in the darkroom
As a picture vivid and bright
Unformed, our very substance
Seen through His marvelous light

Clay formed by the Potter
On the spinning wheel[30]
Shaping the lives of every person
Predestined for His will

Called for such as time as this
To fulfill the purpose of the King
Justified and made righteous
His Son dying to bring

---

28   Genesis 1:26.

29   Psalm 139:13-14.

30   Isaiah 64:8.

Glory to His children
A life of heavenly peace
Dignity and Honor
Struggling has ceased

All of us would like to know
What are we to do?
In the beginning God commanded
Multiply, replenish and subdue[31]

Till the ground, which is under your feet
The purpose to change the earth
Multiply the Word-seed sown
Travailing in the birth

A metamorphosis to everlasting
Stepping out of the norm
Seeing a glimpse of a picture
The life we should conform

Ready and able to be used
For the Master's use[32]
A vessel of honor
Sanctified
Ready to produce

---

31   Genesis 1:28.

32   2 Timothy 2:21.

Not only the fruit of the Spirit
But the gifts that come as well
To build up the kingdom of heaven
To edify and change their well-
To an unblemished cistern[33]
Holding water for a cause
To help the next found kin to inherit
What is found within the clause

You have inherited what is Abraham's
Through Christ, Messiah, the Son
The earth and all that dwells therein
From God, the Father, the Holy One

Interwoven pieces
The body of Messiah tightly knitted
Interwoven lockets
Double knotted, tightly fitted

Chosen as a royal priesthood
Brought together, no worries or cares
Arrayed in beauty
Will stand in unity
Clothed as righteous heirs.

---

33   Matthew 9:17; Proverbs 5:15.

FALL

And another angel came out of the temple, crying
with a loud voice to him that sat on the cloud,
Thrust in thy sickle, and reap: for the time is come
for thee to reap;
for the harvest of the earth is ripe.

—Revelation 14:15

THE ESSENCE OF OUR BEING

What lies in the road ahead,
When all seems none belong?
The quality of our character shows that
Out of our weakness were made strong[34]

Before I move any further,
I'll move from first person to third
So a better understanding can be
made of this poem being heard

She loves the one she follows;
She'll follow him to the valley deep
She encourages his every footstep
To climb that mountain steep

For she knows who holds the keys
To unlock and open every door
For God gives her wisdom
To uphold that man, she does adore

Can you see the twinkle in her eye,
A mist of joy or pain?
Happiness, sorrows, peace, and love
for there's more she can attain

---

34   Hebrews 11:34.

Who can find a virtuous woman?
For her price is far above rubies[35]
Her soul lights up all darkness,
Far beyond the mighty seas

For she knows only what she can bear,
For her soul cries out through the wind
She speaks pure like crystalline diamonds
That often do ascend

Surmounted upon a mountaintop
or found deep within a mine
A diamond in the rough, I tell you,
hold on to what you surely find

Her cry is oh so subtle,
So meek, yet oh so grand
For in the hour of her weakness,
all she can do is just stand

She stands up for Christ's sake,
Making that change in her stride
Moving forward in God's plan,
Not holding onto selfish pride

---

35   Proverbs 31:10.

Strong, mighty, yet humble in spirit,
praying for peace of mind
Women of faith, excellence, destiny, and purpose,
You will undoubtedly find
Every woman is virtuous, I tell you,
look around and you'll see
There are women predestined in serving
The Lord and excelling significantly

The anointing of God has run throughout
Blessing and sanctifying in these days
Worshipping the Lord through our service
To magnify and lift Him up in praise

For every day, this is all,
All that you have been seeing
Seeing the attributes of God move
Through us women, carrying
The Essence of our Being

BELOVED BRETHREN

What kind of men have their hearts set on hope?
To illuminate the treasures from heaven
So others can cope
Cope with the pain that one must obtain
To move closer in God's purpose
To grow spiritually in His name

Men with great demeanor, character,
strength in their eyes
That seek God's face in every aspect of their lives
Lives of struggles, hardships, devastation, and pain
But God will restore to you all the years
That the locust hath eaten[36]
Through Yeshua's name

Men standing in unification
With great purpose and such pride
Receiving a reward if any man's work abide[37]

---

36   Joel 2:25.

37   1 Corinthians 3:14.

For their labor is not in vain
It shall reap with good fruits of the vine
The vine of God's majestic power
Sweeter than aged wine

Beloved brethren, do which is pleasing to God
So your seed can be planted in good soil
That you may be right towards God
So you can be touched with His anointed oil

Praise God from whom all your blessings do flow
For you are highly thought of brethren,
God's gift to the whole world to show

WE ARE

Who are we?
Are we not ourselves?
A peculiar set of people-
Set apart to prevail?
Prevail, oh yes, prevail-
Prevail against the enemy
With one voice
The only choice
Together in harmony
We are like the stars in the sky,
Set up to praise the Most High
We do soar
We do adore
His majestic name
We are like the fire when it blazes,
Like the water when it freezes,
Like the wind as it blows
Do you know?
Do you know?
We are going to illuminate,
cultivate, capture, and achieve
Educate, differentiate all we believe
Believe, who hath believed?
Believed our report?
We stand as capital criminals before
The US Supreme Court
Objection, your Honor
We want to plead our case

We've got souls to save,
People to deliver
From the yolk of bondage they face
Step aside, my brother, my sister
What does this look like to you?
We are the chosen generation
Laborers of the few
We are the generation of Joshua
Entering into the land
Possessing our very promise…
Righteousness
Holiness
Meekness
Temperance
The list goes on and on
On and on
Unified, dignified folk-
This ain't a joke
We must stay alive
And not deprive-
Ourselves of what's ours
We are like explosives
Ready for the spark of light
We sound like thunder
Boom like dynamite
When all is said and done
There is one thing we know
-We are One

Decisions

Which way should I go-
To the left or to the right?
Which way should I go-
To make it through this fight?

A fight of persevering,
Then, the struggles that are ahead,
Because in knowing the decisions that I have made,
I will have to endure these consequences.

Battling between good and evil.
Good will always endure.
The choice is mine to make.

I can't sway,
I can't turn to the left or right-
My thoughts seem uneasy, unstable,
Which way to the light?

Bright burning star that glows with such a warmth,
A feeling of love, charitable grace.

I can't turn around for I decided to make this change,
A geyser of newness has sprung upon me like a leak
That cannot be fixed.

He pours out His ratifying love and comfort
Over my life that I may not sway because
"…God is not the author of
confusion, but of peace…"[38]

---

38   1 Corinthians 14:33.

PRESSING ON

A life with circumstances
Living on second chances
Dare to repeat those things again?
No

But to begin to move toward and face the fight
To have the courage
The strength and might
To press on

The battle within the mind
The kind that moves this flesh to uncertainty
When it starts to speak LOUDLY,
Roaring like a lion
Yet in a cage

Thirst unquenchable until He's near
Panteth after the water brooks, like the deer[39]
When satisfaction only comes
When I hear
His voice speak
Breaking out to being bold, not weak
Needing to seek more
And thus continues on and on
Like a quiet storm
Gathering up the clouds that form
The latter rain anointing

Appointed to a new life
Made it through the hatred and strife
I have pressed on[40]

---

39   Psalm 42:1.

40   Philippians 3:14.

I Knew Thee
Based on 2 Samuel 13 and Ezekiel 16:4–14

John1:1

In the beginning was the Word,
With all power, strength and might-
Before there was a morning,
Before there was a night.

Found in the bod of Jesus,
You and I there lie-
Sanctified and made righteous,
Ordained as we were inside,

Like interwoven pieces,
Sown together with a needle and thread-
Intricately knitted arrayed,
In beauty when God said,

Genesis 1:26
Ps. 139:13–16

Let us make man in our image,
Fearfully and wonderfully made-
Wrought our inward parts,
Under the shadow,
In the shade.

Developed in the darkroom,
As a picture vivid and bright-
Unformed, our very substance,
Seen only through His marvelous light.

2 Cor. 4:7   But we have this treasure in earthen vessels,
Genesis 1:28   Of the dust of the ground we were birthed-
                   Breathes into our nostrils the breath of life,
                   To then multiply and replenish the earth.

2 Samuel 13   Now, the beginning has been told,
                   To reveal this very one-
                   Who had and then a broken vessel,
                   Left to die and left undone.

                   Of this one, she had a treasure,
                   That had a lock and key-
                   Hidden, of diverse colors,
                   To show a belt of chastity.

                   So vexed he was, so sick he became,
                   To love and also woo-
                   And used the time of opportune,
                   To nothing much ado.

                   The outcome told before the act,
                   But had no ear to hear-
                   The spiritual devastation, the hurt inside,
                   To never become My Beloved Dear.

                   Dark shadows cover a once smiling face,
                   Now left to cry and weep-
                   Thy navel cut not from your birth,
                   Left to die in the dark and bleak.

Who would wash you with water,
And swaddle you with bands?
To nurture and protect you
From hurt, harm, and danger,
And keep you from strangers' hands?

No pity could be found at all,
But the One, abundantly He'll give-
While polluted in thine own blood,
With one word He said, "Live!"

A cataclysmic combustion,
Brought back into the light-
Caused to multiply as the bud of the field,
For His enjoyment and delight.

Eccles. 3:2–8   There is a time to be born, a time to mourn,
But the time is now for love-
Covered by an eternal covenant,
Song 2:10   From My Fair One, My Beloved.

Ez. 16:4–14   Clothed with embroidered work from stitchery,
Feet cover with fine leathery seal-
Arrayed in ornaments and fine jewelry,
For His purpose and His will.

Decked out, a crown of glory,
Gold, silver, and fine to eat-
Honey that drips from the honeycomb,
That tastes so very sweet.

Like this one who had a treasure,
Locked up in a chast-
Exceedingly beautiful is now the story,
Of your future, and your past.

Isaiah 43:18   Remember ye not the former things,
Neither consider the things of old-
As He said in the beginning,
Jer. 1:5   Before I formed thee, I knew thee,
Settled, established-
Made righteous-
Pure as gold.

FROM THE MASTER'S TABLE
Based on Matthew 15:21–28 and Mark 7:24–30

One heard of a Savior-
That made straight the crooked street,
Making her way towards to the house-
To fall before His feet.

Matt. 7:6   Not giving that which is holy to dogs,
Not casting pearls before swine,
Yet there's something different,
Unique to know,
When a soul seeks the Divine.

Isa. 41:17   Tongue faileth for thirst-
Soul knocking at His door-
Luke 16:21   Desiring to be fed with the crumbs,
Which fall upon the floor.

Sold into the kingdom-
Bought with a price-
Rev. 21:19   Garnished with a manner of precious stones-
Arrayed in beauty, looking quite nice.
Diamonds, sapphires, rubies, and more-
Ps. 16:11   In His right hand there are pleasures forevermore.

Isaiah 40:11   He feeds His flock like a shepherd-
He gathers the lambs with His arm,
Carrying them within His bosom-
Keeping them safe from all harm.

Luke 22:8   He went ahead to prepare the Passover-
       &   A place where we may eat,
John 14:2   From the land flowing with milk and honey-
            The Everlasting Feast.

Eccles. 10:19   A feast is made for laughter-
            Merry is the heart that findeth the keys,
            Unlocking the hidden treasures of heaven-
            Bowing down on both knees.

            Worship and Praise-
            Giving thanks to the Divine,
            Unblemished cisterns-
Prov. 3:10   Presses burst out with new wine.

            Drinking of the anointing-
            The wine of pure delight-
Eph. 3:18   To comprehend with all saints
            What is the breadth, length, depth, and height.

            The melted blessing conformed to dewdrops-
            That appears in the morn,
            Giving flight to the purpose
            The baby is being born.

Phil. 3:14   Pressing towards the mark-
            Striving to the call,
            Preparing for an elevation-
Ps. 1:3   Changing faith to great from small.

Phil. 4:7   The peace of God passeth all understanding-
Setting the heart as the sun,
Ps. 1:3   Like a tree planted by the rivers of water-
Bringing forth his fruit in his season.

A treasure chosen for a purpose-
Made perfect in His sight,
Zech. 4:6   By my spirit, saith the Lord-
Not by power, nor by might.

Hosea 9:5   What will ye do in the solemn day-?
And in the day of the feast of the Lord?
Are you ready to partake of His goodness-?
To receive the great reward?

Prov. 24:13   Eating of the honey-
Which is sweet to thy taste,
But the sweet has turned bitter-
Which is shown vividly on your face
Are you truly thankful
For Yeshua dying to give you life?
That you may inherit the kingdom of God-
By laying down all manner of strife?

Shall he say,
Matt. 25:21   "Well done, thou good and faithful servant;
Enter thou into the joy of thy Lord,"
Or will you be left wondering-
What haven't I done or ignored?

Shall you continue on?
Having His Spirit to lament?
Wanting you to take hold of the blessing-
If you would only just repent.

The table is set-
Ready for you-
If your soul wishes to be fed-
Or shall you feed upon the crumbs
Where the dog lays its head.

Come up, I say, come up-
If you're willing and truly able,
To take part and eat of The Feast
From the Master's Table.

The Narrow & The Way

Main Scriptures
Psalm 23; Ezekiel 8; Ezekiel 34; John 10;
Matt. 7:13-14; Luke 13:22–30

Psalm 23(NLT)　The Lord IS…my Shepherd
　　　　　　　He showed me in a vision
　　　　　　　The right path He guides
　　　　　　　For His own name's sake
　　　　　　　As the good shepherd and the gate
　　　　　　　To His flock joined as one

　　　　　　　His vision yet clear of green pastures leading
　　　　　　　in peaceful streams
Micah 7:14　　With beams of sunlight rays covering
　　　　　　　the fertile fields & trees of Bashan
　　　　　　　A shalom, a rest in dawn
Psalm 23　　　Through dusk as restored souls

Ezekiel 34:14(NLT) Yes, He gives them good pastureland on the
　　　　　　　high hills of Israel.
　　　　　　　There, they will lie down in pleasant places
　　　　　　　and feed in the lush pastures of the hills.
　　　　　　　And fills their cup to overflowing
Psalm 23:5　　Anointing their heads with oil.

　　　　　　　Blueprints of His top view
　　　　　　　He showed me a terrain of stones
　　　　　　　Fortified like a wall
　　　　　　　To His clarion call

For separation from the outside and others
Gathering in sisters and brothers
Under the anointing of Joseph

He says,

[ACTION]
Raising Moses's staff outward at arm's length

John 10:7	I'M THE GOOD SHEPHERD
	I'M THE GATE FOR THE SHEEP
John 14:6	I'M THE WAY, THE TRUTH
	AND THE LIFE
	Commandments made, KEEP

John 10:7	FOR, I'M THE GOOD SHEPHERD
John 10:3	For, I know you by name
	They hear my voice
	And make the choice
2 Tim. 1:6 (NLT)	The gift to fan into flame

	My Torah, mitzvot, law
	Tablet words on your heart
Isaiah 40:11	Holding you close to comfort
Isaiah 46:10	Declaring finish to the start

[ACTION]
Lower Moses' staff to side

Matt 7:14/John10:9	Safely you enter me into the narrow leads of life
	Now, I, as your bridegroom, and you as my wife

John 10:18   I've laid my life upon the altar as in trade
Psalm 91   And made you to dwell under shadow and shade

       Oh How so beautiful you are
Song 4:1   *Oh How so beautiful you are*
       OH HOW SO BEAUTIFUL YOU ARE
Song 2:10(NLT) Rise up, my darling, fair one,
       Come away with me

Ezekiel 8   So, He took me up to aerial mid
{part of vision} between the earth and the heaven
       To calculate in addition 1 plus 7
       And read
       His Word
       Ezekiel 8
       A large idol at the gate
       Of Temple North
       The inner court
       The entrance to His splendor

       But rend your heart tender, not your garment
       Remove the detestable from my sight
       That stands upright at the entryway to love
       At the entryway of MY love

{part of vision seen} Some have travelled the broad way,
       Alongside to climb this terrain,
       This fence of stone
       But hone into a craft in witch is not me
Ezekiel 8:5   At the gate, they arouse my jealousy
       And believe

Ezekiel 8:12(NLT)   "He doesn't see. He's deserted the land"
Ezekiel 34:3-4   So they feed, and feed, and feed
                    Upon the milk and dress in wool
                    Never to school the weak to strength

                    So, He's calling…*He's calling*
                    HE'S CALLING at great length
                    To say…

[ACTION]
Raising Moses's staff outward at arm's length

Rev. 3:20   **"Here I am. I stand at the door and knock"**
                    Come away, away my people with Israel
John 16:16/   **To one shepherd and one flock**
Ezekiel 34:23

Luke 13:24/   Work hard to enter the narrow way
Matt. 25:21
                    And to enter the joy of Me

Jeremiah 50:19   To feed in the fields of Carmel and Bashan
                    and be satisfied on the hill
                    And I **WILL** the covenant of peace

Matt. 7:14 (TLV)   **How narrow is the gate**
                    And difficult the way that leads to life
                    ….and those who find it are <u>few</u>.

While the earth remaineth, seedtime and harvest,
and cold and heat, and summer and winter,
and day and night shall not cease.

—Genesis 8:22